Challenges for the Delusional

Challenges for the Delusional

Peter Murphy's Prompts
& the Poems They Inspired

edited by Christine Malvasi
assisted by Stephanie Cawley
foreword by Stephen Dunn
introduction by Peter E. Murphy
illustrations by David Sipress

Jane Street Press / NYC
2012

ISBN: 978-0-9723943-8-3

Jane Street Press, 1 Jane Street, Suite 5F, New York, NY 10014, janestreet.org/press.

Murphy Writing Seminars, LLC, 18 N. Richards Ave., Ventnor, NJ 08406, murphywriting.com.

Cover artwork © 2011 by MSzalkowski. Used by permission of Melissa Szalkowski.

Book and cover design: Douglas Goetsch.

Cartoons from *Wishful Thinking* (HarperCollins) by David Sipress. Copyright © 1987 by David Sipress. Used by permission of David Sipress.

*Dedicated to the legions of writers who have attended the Getaway
and the poems they have written there.*

CONTENTS

Foreword

I first met Peter Murphy at the Richard Stockton College of New Jersey in 1974 when I arrived as a writer-in-residence. Peter had just arrived as a student, and while I didn't know his story until later, apparently he had flunked out of three or four colleges in rapid succession before finally winding up at Stockton. Peter was an aspiring poet, earnest and hardworking, but to be honest, I didn't know if he would stick with it. The good news for all of us is that he did.

Peter continued to write poetry and taught creative writing at the high school, college, and graduate levels. Many of his students have begun and continued writing because of his gifted teaching. It is appropriate that this year his annual Winter Poetry & Prose Getaway, where he continues to encourage and teach creative writing, moves to the Seaview Resort, owned by Stockton, where Peter got his start and our friendship began.

Peter's approach to teaching poetry writing is unique and uniquely effective, and his Getaway is a most unusual thing of its kind. I've served as a faculty member at the Getaway for fourteen years, and I've not met anyone who has had less than a wonderful and productive experience. Peter sets a tone that is peculiarly his. It's not that he's more interested in you having fun than in becoming a better writer, it's that the fun he creates for you frequently leads to better writing. His now famous way of beginning each morning at the Getaway is to have several of his faculty read poems that are pertinent to a prompt he has not yet revealed. After we discuss the poems at roundtables he encourages everyone to respond to the prompt by writing a lousy (he uses a different word) poem in two hours. Thus, the onus of excellence is removed. The paradox, of course, is that this approach often leads to excellence.

Kathleen Graber, for example, wrote an extraordinary poem in response to Peter's prompt to include fortune cookie sayings in a poem about aging (see page 45). Kathy is a Getaway success story, having written her very first poem at the Getaway in 1997. In 2010, her second book *The Eternal City* was a finalist for both the National Book Award and the National Book Critics Circle Award.

One of the best Getaway poems I ever got in two hours came from R. G. Evans in response to a prompt with a list of myths and facts about the moon, one of which stated that February 1865 is the only month on record without a full moon. The "challenge for the delusional" was to make it a sonnet, which

ix

Bob did (see page 48).

Even when this approach doesn't lead to a quick success, it still leads to a few good lines, or nothing memorable at all, which doesn't matter; something that might turn out to be a good poem has been set in motion. The challenge, imminent deadline, and permission to make mistakes allow us to discover as we write and move in directions we might not have found otherwise.

You'll see that this anthology is diverse in tone and subject matter, as is fitting to the nature of the Getaway. Peter's quirky prompts have given way to poems that range from humorous to serious, from affectionate to nostalgic. They'll take their place among the workshops, panels, good meals, and late night dancing—the pleasures that abound at the Getaway.

– Stephen Dunn

INTRODUCTION

You need to scrub the kitchen sink. You haven't read all of Dickens or the "Twilight" series. You need to take the dogs and kids for a walk. Don't forget to check them for ticks (the dogs, not the kids, well... maybe) so they don't get sick, or worse, infect you with a horrible disease. You've always wanted to take hip hop lessons or a class on how to make terrariums. And you should buy a new toothbrush because you'll use the one you have to scrub the kitchen sink. How can you possibly concentrate on writing a poem or return to the novel you started last year? Or was it the year before?

I understand. For almost three decades I taught high school English in Atlantic City during the day and composition classes at Richard Stockton College in the evening. I was too exhausted to write during the school year. In the summers, I was fortunate to enjoy residencies at artists' colonies where I could truly concentrate and write poems that surprised and thrilled me. Trouble is, I didn't write the rest of the year.

"Murphy, you phony!" I scolded myself. "You call yourself a writer, but you only write one month a year." So I decided to rent a hotel room and try to recreate my own little Yaddo, at least for a weekend. I left my loved ones at home and shut myself away from everything except Wawa coffee, poetry books I wanted to read, and my laptop (in that order). It worked, so I did it again the next month. And the next. And for more than twenty years I have been writing and revising in hotel rooms, no longer feeling like a hypocrite. When writer friends asked me how I found time to write, I told them, and they kept saying, "I wish I could go with you." After hearing this over and over, in a moment of weakness, I decided to invite them. This was a beautiful mistake.

I called it the Winter Poetry Getaway and reserved a block of rooms at the Grand Hotel in Cape May. I was hoping for a dozen participants and wound up with twenty, so I invited my friend Cat Doty to lead a second feedback session. It was one of the coldest weekends on record, so cold we could hear the ocean freeze! But it was magnificent, and the next year more than thirty people showed up. Some wanted to write stories, so I called it the Winter Poetry (*&* *Prose*) Getaway and brought in more writer friends to help with the workshops. The next year there were forty writers, half of whom were not poets, so I got rid of the parenthesis and the Winter Poetry & Prose Getaway was on its way to becoming one of the largest and most successful writing conferences in the country. It regularly attracts over 200 writers and has led me to run other getaways throughout the year, including writing retreats in New Hampshire and in Wales.

Now, the Getaway is entering its nineteenth year, its last year as a teenager. It has moved out of its childhood home and moved into the Seaview Resort in partnership with Stockton. As we load the SUV, we want to collect our photographs, or at least our prompts and poems, in the spirit of remembering, celebrating, and looking forward to what's next.

Part one of this anthology features writing assignments selected from the first eighteen years. Here's how it works. We gather the poets together each morning to discuss a small collection of poems before I give one of my legendary prompts and send everyone off to write a "shitty first draft" in two hours. "Don't worry," I say, "you'll revise it later." The point is, if you don't allow yourself to write badly, you'll never write well.

After lunch, the poets and their baby drafts report to supportive workshop sessions led by carefully handpicked writer-teachers who encourage the poems' virtues while helping the poets recognize and eliminate what doesn't work.

My prompts are designed to trick you into writing a poem you didn't know you could write. They offer a set of specific requirements along with a general theme. For example, one asks you to drop an insect (or a couple billion insects) into a poem about forgiveness. While you're bogged down on including the bugs, your subconscious will go to work on the real material of the poem, allowing its true subject to bubble up in an interesting way. Another requirement is to "tell a secret, tell a lie and never tell anyone which is which." The secret forces you to create intimacy. The lie gives you permission to imagine what you might not have otherwise. The goal is to discover something you might not have already known, something that will surprise you and resonate with a reader.

Most prompts include variations on the theme. For example, if you don't want your insects hatching in a poem about forgiveness, try revenge instead. If you're feeling particularly adventurous, you might want to attempt the "challenge for the delusional," which in this case is to write your poem from the point of view of an insect. You'll find whatever quotations, fortunes, and facts (like the names of creepy-crawlies) that you might need in the appendix or at murphywriting.com/anthology. Finally, the prompts list poems that might nudge you in an interesting direction. Seek out these poems on your own to see what they might stir up.

Part two of this anthology features a selection of poems inspired by the prompts. Don't try too hard to match them since many of the poems have been revised away from their original genesis. I hope that you'll enjoy this small sampling of poems as representative of a larger body of strong, Getaway-inspired writing. Whether you are new to the Getaway or are a re-PETER, *do* try this at home. Grab some paper and a prompt. Let this anthology encourage you to put down that sink-scrubbing toothbrush and pick up a pencil instead.

– Peter E. Murphy

PROMPTS

Humor and Heteronyms
5ᵗʰ Annual Getaway, 1998

Assignment: Write a poem that uses humor in an unexpected way.

Requirements:

1) Exaggerate a personal quirk or character flaw.
2) Refer to a historical disaster (sorry, no Titanics allowed!)
3) Include a heteronym. (Heteronyms are words that are spelled the same but have different pronunciations and meanings.) Here is my personal list: abuse, address, alternate, axes, bass, bow, can, close, conduct, convict, defect, desert, dove, excuse, invalid, Job, lead, live, minute, object, offense, Polish, present, read, record, refuse, resume, tear, wind, wound.

Can you add to it?

Challenge for the delusional: "I say drop a mouse into a poem." – Billy Collins

Poems to reference:

"Introduction to Poetry," by Billy Collins. *The Apple That Astonished Paris,* 1988.
"Poem [Lana Turner has collapsed!]," by Frank O'Hara. *Lunch Poems,* 1964.
"(may i feel said he)," by e.e. cummings. *100 Selected Poems,* 1926.
"wishes for sons," and "to my last period" by Lucille Clifton. *Quilting: Poems 1987 – 1990,* 1991.
"The Feet Man," by Philip Dacey. *Night Shift at the Crucifix Factory,* 1991.
"The One That Got Away," by Gary Miranda. *Listeners at the Breathing Place,* 1978.
"Did I Miss Anything?" by Tom Wayman. *The Astonishing Weight of the Dead,* 1994.
"The Bagel" and "Self-Employed," by David Ignatow. *Rescue the Dead,* 1968.

* * *

Surprise yourself! Do not settle for what you already know!

Elegiacal Boggle
6ᵗʰ Annual Getaway, 1999

―――――――――

Assignment: Write an elegy, which is a poem of lament and praise for the dead, for someone either notorious or famous, whom you admire or abhor.

Variation: Write an elegy for yourself. Reveal a secret and tell a lie, and do not tell anyone which is which, ever!

Warning: Do Not Write a Bad Elegy!

Requirements:

1) Find your own quotation, relic, picture, or literary memento and insinuate it in the poem.
2) Include eight words from Karen Banks' Boggle list:* here, every, save, past, east, very, home, saver, vast, mess, seas, some, saves, seer, fast, most, pass, peas, espy, heap, heaps, homes—or create a Boggle list of your own.

Challenge for the delusional: Use three of the ten words again as homonyms. (Homonyms are words that are spelled and sound the same but have different meanings.)

Poems to reference:

"Little Elegy," by Keith Althaus. *Ladder of Hours*, 2005.
"My Father's Hobby," by Morton Marcus. *Moments Without Names: New and Selected Prose Poems,* 2002.
"Childlessness," by Henri Cole. *The Look of Things*, 1995.
"Elegy," by Larry Levis. *The Afterlife,* 1998.
"Lilacs for Ginsberg," by Gerald Stern. *This Time: New and Selected Poems,* 1998.
"Hitler's First Photograph," by Wislawa Szymborska. *View With a Grain of Sand,* 1993.
"Ashes [My left hand joggled Johnny's arm]," by Andrew Hudgins. *Babylon in a Jar,* 1998.

* * *

Surprise yourself! Do not settle for what you already know!

―――――――――

* Karen Banks played a mean game of Boggle at the fifth getaway. When she couldn't make it to the sixth, we wanted her to feel included by having her Boggle lists featured in that year's set of prompts.

18

Aging Fortune Cookies
9th Annual Getaway, 2002

Now I'm growing up.
Year after year after year after year,
  Age steps upon me.
    – Steven Watson, aged 13

But at my back I always hear
Time's wingèd chariot hurrying near;
And yonder all before us lie
Deserts of vast eternity.
    – Andrew Marvell, dead

Assignment: Write a poem about Aging. While it seems that we age more quickly as we get older, aging is not restricted to the sunset years of our lives.

Requirements: Use a fortune cookie saying (or several) in your poem (see Appendix A for a list of fortunes). You may quote it, refer to it, reverse it, argue it, or dismiss it, but try to get it in. The fortune doesn't have to have anything to do with aging.

Variation: Like the Cassian poem, write it "the other way around," i.e., write about "youthing" instead of aging.

Challenge for the delusional: Refer to, respond to or argue against one of the random quotations in Appendix A.

Poems to reference:

"Men at Forty," by Donald Justice. *Night Light,* 1967.
"Grandmother Love Poem," by Sharon Olds. *The Dead and the Living,* 1983.
"High Windows," by Philip Larkin. *High Windows,* 1974.
"Fifteen," by William Stafford. *The Darkness Around Us Is Deep: Selected Poems of William Stafford,* 1993.
"Youthing," by Nina Cassian. *The Atlantic Monthly,* Vol. 280, No. 4, October 1997.
"The Diagnosis," by James Tate. *The Best American Poetry,* Robert Hass and David Lehman, eds., 2001.

* * *

Tell a secret. Tell a lie. Surprise yourself!
Do not settle for what you already know.

Postcard-sized Apology
9th Annual Getaway, 2002

"Love means never having to say you're sorry."
– *Love Story, 1970*

Assignment: Write a postcard-sized poem in which you apologize for or argue against something or someone for an offense, real or imagined.

Requirements: Choose three postcards that attract you and one that disgusts or confuses you, and incorporate one or more of these images into your poem.*

Variation: Have someone apologize to you instead. Wouldn't that be sweet?

Challenge for the delusional: C'mon, do you really need any more stimulation? Oh, all right. Integrate some writing from one or more of the postcards into your poem.

Poems to reference:

"Why I Never Came," by Renée Ashley. *The Various Reasons of Light,* 1998.
"An Argument: On 1942," by David Mura. *After We Lost Our Way,* 1989.

* * *

Surprise yourself! Yeah! Yeah! Yeah!

---

* At the Getaway we supply a pile of postcards to choose from. Find one of your own or sort through old photographs or letters. You could also search online for Google images or through our virtual postcard collection at murphywriting.com/anthology.

Making and Unmaking
9th Annual Getaway, 2002

---

po· em (Gr. *poiein*, to make) *n*. Anything made, especially an arrangement of words having beauty of thought or language.

Assignment: Write a poem about Making something. Your "made thing" should be about something physical, which may resonate with metaphor.

Requirement: Use a random quotation into your poem (see Appendix A). You may quote it, refer to it, reverse it, argue it, or dismiss it, but try to get it in.

Variation: Write a poem about "unmaking." It can be the unraveling of a "thing" or a life or an idea.

Challenge for the delusional: Infuse a fortune or two in addition to one of the random quotations in Appendix A.

Poems to reference:

"A Theory of Prosody," by Philip Levine. *A Walk with Tom Jefferson,* 1988.

"Carpenter of the Sun," by Nancy Willard. *Carpenter of the Sun,* 1974.

"What the Gypsies Told My Grandmother While She Was Still a Young Girl," by Charles Simic. *Walking the Black Cat,* 1996.

"Anon," by Linda Pastan. *Witness,* Vol. 11, No. 2, 1997.

"Plague Victims Catapulted over Walls into Besieged City," by Thomas Lux. *The Street of Clocks,* 2001.

"How I Got Born," "Who Am I?" and "My Heart," by Cornelius Eady. *Brutal Imagination,* 2001.

Joisey
10ᵗʰ Annual Getaway, 2003

"Susan, we thought you wuz dead. *I was. I was in Joisey.*"
– *Desperately Seeking Susan*

"Not going to New Jersey isn't procrastinating. It's common sense."
– *Igby Goes Down*

Assignment: Write a poem about New Jersey, real or imagined. Refer to the whole state or to just one part of it that you find weird, wired or wonderful. Consider the difference between the typical and the stereotypical New Jersey. Name names. Be specific and visionary.

Requirement: Support, repeat or argue against one or more of the items from the "New Jersey Facts and Trivia" list in Appendix B. Or find your own New Jersey facts.

Variation: Write about another state (or city or place) that you may know better or have more attitude about. OR Warp it. Personify New Jersey so it fights back, talks trash to New York, Pennsylvania and its other vain siblings.

Challenge for the delusional: Refer to a New Jersey joke or movie quotation in your poem.*

Poems to reference:

"Far Away," by Jane Miller. *Memory at These Speeds: New and Selected Poems,* 1996.
"Stendhal in Sea Isle City," by Stephen Dunn. *Local Visitations,* 2003.
"The Simple Truth," by Philip Levine. *The Simple Truth,* 1994.
"Jersey Lyric," by William Carlos Williams. *Collected Poems of William Carlos Williams, Vol. 2: 1939 – 1962,* 1988.
"Lilith," by Enid Dame. Lilith and Her Demons, 1989.
"New Jersey," by BJ Ward. Gravedigger's Birthday, 2002.
"The Invention of New Jersey," by Jack Anderson. Selected Poems, 1983.

---

* Or TV show quotation. Since this prompt was written, plenty of conspicuous New Jersey-themed shows have made their way into our reality.

Your Name Here
10th Annual Getaway, 2003

O Romeo, Romeo! wherefore art thou Romeo?
Deny thy father and refuse thy name...
'Tis but thy name that is my enemy...
What's in a name? that which we call a rose
By any other name would smell as sweet.
    – *Romeo and Juliet* (II.ii.33-44)

Assignment: Write a poem in which you invoke your own name—first, last, middle or "nick." You can write your poem in the first person, the second person, the third person, or in both first and third person like César Vallejo. Think of others in your life or in history who have shared your name and see if they would like to be in your draft. Your poem doesn't have to be autobiographical, but it may refer to the events or concerns of your own life. Feel free to include something about the meaning or origin of your name. If your name doesn't have a particular meaning or you don't know its etymology, make it up.

Requirement: Support, repeat or argue against one or more of the "Truth, Lies and Honesty" quotations in Appendix B.

Variation: Write about names like Hayden, or invoke another, more famous name like O'Hara. OR Use your Secret Name, the one only you know and answer to, or make up a new name for yourself and write about that one instead.

Challenge for the delusional: Write in form. Try a ghazal, pantoum, sestina, sonnet or villanelle.

Poems to reference:

"Names," by Robert Hayden. *Collected Poems of Robert Hayden,* 1985.
"Ghazal," by Agha Shahid Ali. *The Country Without a Post Office,* 1997.
"Don't Kill Yourself," by Carlos Drummond de Andrade (Translated by Mark Strand). *Another Republic,* 1976.
"What Zimmer Would Be," by Paul Zimmer. *The Zimmer Poems,* 1976.
"Black Stone Lying On A White Stone," by César Vallejo (Translated by Robert Bly). *Neruda & Vallejo: Selected Poems,* 1971.
"Charles Simic," by Charles Simic. *Return to a Place Lit by a Glass of Milk,* 1974.
"Night Mirror," by Li-Young Lee. *Book of My Nights,* 2001.

Time and Again
11ᵗʰ Annual Getaway, 2004

"Had we but world enough, and time,
  This coyness, Lady, were no crime...."
  – *Andrew Marvell*

"Time flies like an arrow; fruit flies like a banana."
  – *Groucho Marx*

"I've been on a calendar, but I have never been on time."
  – *Marilyn Monroe*

Assignment: Write a poem about Time in which you question or challenge an important personal relationship.

Requirement: Refer to, support, repeat, adapt or argue against one or more of the "Time" quotations in Appendix C.

Variation: Write about one of the clichés below to make it original again.

All in due time; He doesn't know what time it is; In the nick of time; Marking time; A stitch in time saves nine; Time after time; Time and again; Time flies when you're having fun; Time heals all wounds; Time is running out; Time on your hands; The times, they are a changing

Challenge for the delusional: Refer to, support, repeat, adapt or argue against one or more of the "Einstein Says..." quotations in Appendix C.

Poems to reference:

"I Haven't Got All Day," by Sharon Bryan. *Flying Blind,* 1996.
"Monet's 'Waterlilies,'" by Robert Hayden. *Collected Poems of Robert Hayden,* 1985.
"Today," by Catherine Doty. *Momentum,* 2004.
"After a Long Time Away," by Patrick Donnelly. *The Charge,* 2003.
"The Last Time," by Marie Howe. *What the Living Do,* 1998.
"Growth," by Brian Johnstone. *Sou'wester,* 2002.
"Watchmaker's Insomnia," by Benjamin Paloff. *The New Republic,* December 2003.
"The Change," by Tony Hoagland. *What Narcissism Means to Me,* 2003.

Another Prompt, Another Dollar
11th Annual Getaway, 2004

───────────

"Money is better than poverty, if only for financial reasons."
  – *Woody Allen*

"The more money people have, the less they sing."
  – *Unknown*

"The trick is to stop thinking of it as your money."
  – *IRS auditor*

Assignment: Write a poem about Money or any of its cousins (wealth, cash, currency, loot, capital, riches, treasure, etc.).

Requirement: Refer to, support, repeat, adapt or argue against one or more of the "Money" quotations in Appendix D.

Variation: Write about the joys of poverty. How does the term "Starving Artist" refer to you?

Challenge for the delusional: Use "money" words that exploit non-financial meanings, e.g., bank, interest, taxing, save, economy, spent, deduction, quotation, and strike.

Poems to reference:

  "Money," by Dana Gioia. *The Gods of Winter,* 1991.
  "Money Can't Fix It," by Terese Svoboda. *Treason,* 2002.
  "After Hearing a Radio Announcement," by Quincy Troupe. *Transcircularities: New and Selected Poems,* 2002.
  "A Minor Riot at the Mint," by Natasha Sajé. *Bend,* 2003.
  "Sunday in Glastonbury," by Robert Bly. *Contemporary American Poetry,* Donald Hall, ed., 1972.
  "$" by Carol Ann Duffy. *Standing Female Nude,* 1985.
  "Time Is Money," by Sidney Wade. *Celestial Bodies,* 2002.

Blessed or Cursed
11ᵗʰ Annual Getaway, 2004

"May the road rise to meet you.
  May the wind be always at your back."
    – an Irish blessing

Assignment: Write a postcard-sized poem that blesses someone or something.

Requirements: Choose three postcards that attract you and one that disgusts or confuses you, and incorporate some of these images into your poem.*

Variation: Write to yourself as someone you wish would offer you a blessing. Wouldn't that be sweet? OR Forget the blessing. Write a curse!

Challenge for the delusional: C'mon, do you really need any more stimulation? Oh, all right. Integrate some writing from one or more of the postcards into your poem.

Poems to reference:

"A Blessing," by James Wright. *Selected Poems,* 2005.
"Traveller's Curse after Misdirection (from the Welsh)," by Robert Graves. *The Complete Poems in One Volume,* 2001.
"In a Dark Time Together," by Mary Ann Samyn. *Beauty Breaks In,* 2009.

---

* You could search online through our virtual postcard collection at murphywriting.com/anthology.

The Tube
12th Annual Getaway, 2005

"Television enables you to be entertained in your home by people
   you wouldn't have in your home."
   – *David Frost*

"Imitation is the sincerest form of television."
   – *Fred Allen*

"I hate entertainment. Entertainment is a thing of the past, now
   we got television."
   – *Archie Bunker*

Assignment: Write a love poem for Television. Okay, it can be a hate poem instead, but write beyond or beneath what's apparent.

Requirement: Refer to, include, swipe, steal, amend or argue against one or more of the "Television" quotations in Appendix D. Be specific. Name names and quote quotes from your television memory.

Variation: Write the poem from the point of view of a television character or celebrity.

Challenge for the delusional: Include a jingle or theme song or some other television music, jargon or slogan.

Poems to reference:

"A Singular Metamorphosis" by Howard Nemerov. *The Collected Poems of Howard Nemerov,* 1981.
"Snow Globe," by Kim Addonizio. *Ploughshares,* Spring 1998.
"To Television," by Robert Pinsky. *Jersey Rain,* 2000.
"Philly in the Light," by Honorée Fanonne Jeffers. *The Gospel of Barbecue,* 2000.
"Hearings," by Tony Hoagland. *Donkey Gospel,* 1998.
"How the Sky Fell," by Denise Duhamel. *How The Sky Fell,* 1996.
"The Insistence of Beauty," by Stephen Dunn. *The Insistence of Beauty,* 2004.

The Odyssey
13th Annual Getaway, 2006

"Too often travel, instead of broadening the mind, merely lengthens the conversation."
 – *Elizabeth Drew*

"If God had really intended men to fly, he'd make it easier to get to the airport."
 – *George Winters*

"It is not worth the while to go around the world to count the cats in Zanzibar."
 – *Henry David Thoreau*

Assignment: Write a poem in which you journey, either outward or inward. You can contrive an imaginary destination or trip to the future or the past.

Requirements:

1) Integrate one or more of "The Odyssey" quotations in Appendix E into your poem. Feel free to slaughter them.
2) Borrow and alter a line or image from one of the poems listed below.
3) Use exotic action verbs.

Variations: "Speak, Knees...." Choose a body part to narrate your odyssey. OR Write an agoraphobic poem. Invent ridiculous excuses for going nowhere.

Challenge for the delusional: Make it a sonnet.

Poems to reference:

"Speak, Memory," by Homer (Translated by Stanley Lombardo). *The Odyssey,* 2000.
"N," by Maurya Simon. *Speaking in Tongues,* 1990.
"A Supermarket in California," by Allen Ginsberg. *Collected Poems: 1947 – 1980,* 1988.
"Travel Plans," by Leslie Monsour. *The Alarming Beauty of the Sky,* 2005.
"The Strange Hours Travelers Keep," by August Kleinzahler. *The Strange Hours Travelers Keep,* 2003.
"Odyssey," by Bob Hicok. *The American Poetry Review,* September/October 2005.
"Making a Fist," by Naomi Shihab Nye. *Words Under the Words: Selected Poems,* 1995.
"Traveling Alone," by Billy Collins. *The Trouble with Poetry,* 2005.
"Widow," by Vénus Khoury-Ghata (Translated by Marilyn Hacker). *Here There Was Once a Country,* 2001.

Keep Making Excuses
13ᵗʰ Annual Getaway, 2006

"He that is good for making excuses is seldom good for anything else."
  – *Benjamin Franklin*

"If I remember right there are five excuses for drinking: the visit of a guest, present thirst, future thirst, the goodness of the wine, and any other excuse you choose!"
  – *Pete Sermond*

"The day you take complete responsibility for yourself, the day you stop making any excuses, that's the day you start to the top."
  – *O. J. Simpson*

Assignment: Write a postcard-sized poem in which you write an outrageous excuse.

Requirements: Choose three postcards that attract you and one that disturbs or confuses you, and incorporate some of these images into your poem.*

Variation: Instead of an excuse, your poem may brag about or confess to unimaginable crimes so heinous they would shock Jerry Springer.

Challenge for the delusional: Integrate writing from one or more of the postcards into your poem.

Poems to reference:

 "This is Just to Say," by William Carlos Williams. *The Collected Poems of William Carlos Williams, Vol. 1: 1909 – 1939,* 1991.
 "Variations on a Theme by William Carlos Williams," by Kenneth Koch. *Thank You, and Other Poems,* 1962.

---

* You could search online through our virtual postcard collection at murphywriting.com/anthology.

To the Moon
14th Annual Getaway, 2007

"Lunarian, an inhabitant of the moon, as distinguished from Lunatic, one whom the moon inhabits."
  – *Ambrose Bierce*

"There are nights when the wolves are silent and only the moon howls."
  – *George Carlin*

Assignment: Write a poem about the Moon, real or imagined, in which you question or challenge a difficult personal relationship.

Requirements:

1) Refer to one or two myths, facts or phrases about the moon and/or an O'Neill quotation or a combination of both (see Appendix F).
2) Tell a secret and tell a lie and never tell anyone which is which.
3) Pay attention to the music of the poem. Make it sound good.

Variation: Write from the point of view of the moon lamenting your wonderful, pitiful life. Have the moon howl!

Challenge for the delusional: Make it a sonnet.

Poems to reference:

"The Missing Always Leave Something Behind," by Jen Town. *Cimarron Review,* No. 155, Spring 2006.
"Song," by Priscilla Sneff. *The Kenyon Review,* Vol. 27, No. 2, Spring 2005.
"My First Love Was a Plover," by Twm Morys. *Ofn Fy Het (Afraid of My Hat),* 1995.
"One Night in the 7-Eleven," by Eleanor Lerman. *The Mystery of Meteors,* 2001.
"The Stars Are," by Samuel Menashe. *Poetry,* September 2004.
"Midnight Ceremony," by Lisa Furmanski. *Beloit Poetry Journal,* Vol. 54, No. 4, Summer 2004.
"The World is Too Much With Us," by William Wordsworth. *Poems, in Two Volumes,* 1807.

Give Birth to Yourself
14th Annual Getaway, 2007

"Your birth is a mistake you'll spend your whole life trying to correct."
  – *Chuck Palahniuk*

"Man's main task is to give birth to himself."
  – *Erich Fromm*

"Somewhere on this globe, every ten seconds, there is a woman giving birth to a child. She must be found and stopped."
  – *Sam Levenson*

Assignment: Write a postcard-sized poem in which you "give birth to yourself." This could be about your actual birth or it could be an imaginary one, perhaps the one you wish you had.

Requirements:

1) Choose three postcards that attract you and one that disturbs or confuses you, and incorporate some of these images into your poem.*
2) Mention a specific geographical location.

Variation: Instead of your own birth, you can sit in on the birth of a literary or historical figure and write about that.

Challenge for the delusional: Steal writing from one or more of the postcards and use it in your poem.

Poems to reference:

"Born in the U.S.A.," by Bruce Springsteen. *Born in the U.S.A.,* 1984.
"Born in the U.K.," by Badly Drawn Boy. *Born in the U.K.,* 2006.
"A Report to an Academy," by Joel Brouwer. *Poetry,* December 2006.
"Returning Home after the Birth of My Son," by Kip Knott. *Mudlark,* No. 26, 2004.

---

* You could search online through our virtual postcard collection at murphywriting.com/anthology.

Mistakes You Don't Regret
15ᵗʰ Annual Getaway, 2008

_____

"Some of the worst mistakes of my life have been haircuts."
  – Jim Morrison

"Football is a mistake. It combines the two worst elements of American life:
violence and committee meetings."
  – George F. Will

"It is a mistake to think you can solve any major problems just with potatoes."
  – Douglas Adams

Assignment: Write a poem about a mistake you do not regret.

Requirements:

  1) Include a curse, as creative as you can get away with.
  2) Allude to or borrow one of the "My bad" quotations in Appendix G.

Variations: Write about a historical or scientific mistake instead of a personal one, but make it intimate.

Challenge for the delusional: Write a sonnet or villanelle with all the twists and turns you can manage without making too many mistakes.

Poems to reference:

"Variations on a Theme by William Carlos Williams," by Kenneth Koch. *Thank You, and Other Poems,* 1962.
"The Man Who Wouldn't Plant Willow Trees," by A. E. Stallings. *Archaic Smile: Poems,* 1999.
"Lying in a Hammock at William Duffy's Farm in Pine Island, Minnesota," by James Wright. *Collected Poems,* 1971.
"The Bean Eaters," by Gwendolyn Brooks. *The Bean Eaters,* 1960.
"Cold Spring," by Lawrence Raab. *Other Children,* 1987.
"Poem [Lana Turner has collapsed!]," by Frank O'Hara. *Lunch Poems,* 1964.
"The Bagel," by David Ignatow. *Rescue the Dead,* 1968.
"Afraid So," by Jeanne Marie Beaumont. *Curious Conduct,* 2004.

Success or Failure
16th Annual Getaway, 2009

"There's no secret about success. Did you ever know a successful man
who didn't tell you about it?"
  – Kin Hubbard

"In Hollywood a marriage is a success if it outlasts milk."
  – Rita Rudner

Assignment: Drop a large body of water into a poem about Success or Failure.

Requirements:

  1) Allude to or borrow one of the "Success/Failure" quotations in Appendix G.
  2) Invigorate the music of the poem.
  3) Tell a secret, tell a lie and never tell anyone which is which.

Variation: Okay, you might suffer from hydrophobia... uh, no, that's rabies.
Nonetheless, you might want to avoid H_2O. Instead drop a large landmass—
desert, forest, mountain range, shopping mall, etc.—into your poem.

Challenge for the delusional: Write an iconographic poem à la May Swenson. OR
What the hell... Hades. Refer to your favorite mythological figure.

Poems to reference:

"The United States," by C. K. Williams. *Wait,* 2010.
"Undertow," by Dean Young. *Poetry,* November 2007.
"How Everything Happens (Based on a Study of the Wave)," by May Swenson.
  Iconographs, 1970.
"And Soul," by Eavan Boland. *Domestic Violence,* 2007.
"Checkmate," by Lucio Mariani (Translated by Anthony Molino). *Echoes of
  Memory,* 2003.
"Odysseus Hears of the Death of Kalypso," by Donald Revell. *Poetry,* June 2008.
"Of Politics, & Art," by Norman Dubie. *The Mercy Seat: New and Selected Poems
  1967 – 2000,* 2000.
"Failure," by Philip Schultz. *Failure,* 2007.
"Learning to Love America," by Shirley Geok-lin Lim. *What the Fortune Teller
  Didn't Say,* 1998.

The Art of Translation
16th Annual Getaway, 2009

———————

Assignment: Find a poem written in a language that you don't know. "Translate" it into a postcard-sized poem that mimics the form of the original poem. For example, if the original poem is in couplets with short lines, write your poem in couplets with short lines.

As for your translation, you may simply guess at the words' meanings (using a dictionary is no fun) or attempt a "homophonic translation," "translating" the foreign words into English words that you think sound the same. In other words, just make up something that looks like it could be a translation.*

Requirements:

1) Choose three postcards that attract you and one that disturbs or confuses you, and integrate some of these images into your poem.**
2) Pay attention to the repetitions, sounds, and rhythms of the original poem and imitate them in your poem.

Variation: Give your poem a strange title.

Challenge for the delusional: Steal writing from one or more of the postcards and use it in your poem.

Poems to reference:

"Deall Goleuni" ("Understanding Light") by Elin Ap Hywel. *Oxygen: New Poets from Wales,* 2000.

"Adduned" ("Pledge") by Gerwyn Williams. *Oxygen: New Poets from Wales,* 2000.

———————

* At the Getaway we featured the poem "Adduned," by Welsh poet Gerwyn Williams ("Oherwydd dy ddodi'n fy mreichiau, / yn amddiafad 'rôl magwrfa'r groth; // oherwydd dy wythbwys....") and asked participants to "translate" it. The "variation" was to give your poem a strange title such as "Scrubs," "Wood Splendor," "Old English," "Lemon Oil" or "Murphy Soap." Look up that poem or find another to "translate" on your own.

** You could search online through our virtual postcard collection at murphywriting.com/anthology.

Dancing and Death
17th Annual Getaway, 2010

———————

"Angels dancing on the head of a pin dissolve into nothingness at the bedside of a dying child."
   – Waiter Rant weblog (waiterrant.net), June 21, 2005

"There is nothing more notable in Socrates than that he found time, when he was an old man, to learn music and dancing, and thought it time well spent."
   – Michel de Montaigne

"You need chaos in your soul to give birth to a dancing star."
   – Friedrich Nietzsche

Assignment: Get some dancing into a poem that touches death.

Requirements:

1) Use action verbs and concrete nouns to create a frenzy of chaos.
2) Include language from "Random Dance Terms" in Appendix H.
3) Tell a secret, tell a lie and never tell anyone which is which.

Variation: Write a poem unrelated to dancing, but using language from "Random Dance Terms" in a non-contextual way.

Challenge for the delusional: Make your poem sound or move like it's dancing.

Poems to reference:

"American Smooth," by Rita Dove. *American Smooth,* 2004.
"Tarantula, or The Dance of Death," by Anthony Hecht. *Collected Earlier Poems,* 1990.
"Gym Dance with the Doors Wide Open," by J. Allyn Rosser. *Poetry,* May 2006.
"Buddha with a Cell Phone," by David Romtvedt. *Some Church,* 2005.
"Dance the Orange," by Rainer Maria Rilke (Translated by A. Poulin, Jr.). *Duino Elegies and The Sonnets to Orpheus,* 1977.
"Danse Russe," by William Carlos Williams. *The Collected Poems of William Carlos Williams, Vol. 2: 1939 – 1962,* 1991.
"The Bald Headed Doll," by Hal Sirowitz. *Father Said,* 2004.
"Wedding Piñata," by James Hoch. *Copper Nickel,* 2009.
"The Edge," by Bob Hicok. *The Iowa Review,* Vol. 32, No. 1, Spring 2002.

Clown Wisdom
17th Annual Getaway, 2010

"The energy in a pair of shoes at rest / Is about the same as that of a clown //
Knocked flat by a sandbag."
    – *Cornelius Eady*

"The artist, like the idiot or clown, sits on the edge of the world, and a push may
send him over it."
    – *Osbert Sitwell*

"Clowns to the left of me, jokers to the right. Here I am, stuck in the middle with
you."
    – *Stealers Wheel*

Assignment: Write a poem celebrating something or someone unlikely to ever
have been celebrated before.

Requirements:

1) Drop a clown into your poem and/or include language from "Clown
    Wisdom" in Appendix I.
2) Use repetition repeatedly without tiring the reader or yourself.
3) Tell a secret, tell a lie and never tell anyone which is which.

Variation: Address your poem to a clown or a politician.

Challenge for the delusional: Be funny!

Poems to reference:

"Passing Through," by Stanley Kunitz. *The Collected Poems of Stanley Kunitz,*
    2000.
"won't you celebrate with me," by Lucille Clifton. *The Book of Light,* 1993.
"Dangerous Astronomy," by Sherman Alexie. *Face,* 2009.
"The Horse Fell Off the Poem," by Mahmoud Darwish (Translated by Fady
    Joudah). *The Butterfly's Burden,* 2006.
"Jet," by Tony Hoagland. *Donkey Gospel,* 1998.
"The Cossacks," by Linda Pastan. *The Last Uncle,* 2002.
"No Palms," by Dorothea Tanning. *A Table of Content,* 2004.
"Meditation at Lagunitas," by Robert Hass. *Praise,* 1979.
"If a Clown," by Stephen Dunn. *Here and Now: Poems,* 2011.

Forgiveness and Creepy-Crawlies
18ᵗʰ Annual Getaway, 2011

"Nothing inspires forgiveness quite like revenge."
  – *Scott Adams*

"It is easier to get forgiveness than permission."
  – *Murphy's Law*

Assignment: Drop an insect (or a couple billion insects) into a poem about Forgiveness.

Requirements:

1) Try not to mention forgiveness or any of its cousins: compassion, charity, pity, mercy, favor, grace, kindness, clemency, leniency, benevolence, or forbearance. Instead, create language to show it in an original way.
2) Find something interesting from the list of "Insect Common Names" in Appendix J.
3) Tell a secret, tell a lie and never tell anyone which is which.

Variation: Drop insects into a poem about revenge instead.

Challenge for the delusional: Write your poem from the point of view of a creepy-crawly.

Poems to reference:

"Design," by Robert Frost. *The Poetry of Robert Frost,* 1969.
"Whatever Can Be Done, Will Be Done," by Constance Urdang. *The Picnic in the Cemetery,* 1975.
"Eating Alone," by Li-Young Lee. *Rose,* 1986.
"On Distinction," by A. F. Moritz. *Rest on the Flight into Egypt,* 1999.
"Feeling Sorry for Myself While Standing Before the Stegosaurus at the Natural History Museum in London," by Michael Derrick Hudson. *New Ohio Review,* No. 8, Fall 2010.
"Weaponry," by Kim Addonizio. *Lucifer at the Starlite,* 2009.
"The Pear," by Jane Hirshfield. *Come, Thief,* 2011.
"With Mercy for the Greedy," by Anne Sexton. *The Complete Poems of Anne Sexton,* 1981.

The Furniture in Heaven
18th Annual Getaway, 2011

"In heaven all the interesting people are missing."
– *Friedrich Nietzsche*

"The only paradise is paradise lost."
– *Marcel Proust*

Assignment: Put furniture into a poem about heaven.

Requirements:

1) Try to create an original metaphor, the way "couch potato" was once original.
2) Furnish your poem with language from the "Furniture" list in Appendix K.
3) Tell a secret, tell a lie and never tell anyone which is which.

Variation: Okay, it's Sunday and Ikea is closed. Drive a vehicle into heaven instead.

Challenge for the delusional: Make heaven more interesting than hell.

Poems to reference:

"Spaces We Leave Empty," by Cathy Song. *Picture Bride,* 1983.
"Heaven of Animals," by James Dickey. *Poems 1957 – 1967,* 1967.
"A High-Toned Old Christian Woman," by Wallace Stevens. *Collected Poems,* 1954.
"Heaven to Be," by Sharon Olds. *Strike Sparks: Selected Poems 1980 – 2002,* 2004.
"Wanting Sumptuous Heavens," by Robert Bly. *The New Yorker,* November 5, 2007.
"Testimonial," by Rita Dove. *On the Bus with Rosa Parks,* 1999.
"here rests," by Lucille Clifton. *Mercy,* 2004.
"Broken Promises," by David Kirby. *Big-leg Music,* 1995.
"[Of a girl, in white]," by Harryette Mullen. *Recyclopedia,* 2006.

POEMS

Follen Street
Laure-Anne Bosselaar

I do it each time we move, do it
again to our new house in this listless
Cambridge street:

press my forehead and palms
to the door, ask *Forgive me* before
I bring in my mess: relics,

hopes, insomnia, clocks.
Then, while the man I love carefully
prints our names on the mailbox,

I chase vacancy away with broom
and books, hang the paintings—those fake
windows I need

to comfort me from what I keep
seeing through lucid ones: the same skies,
traffic, worn-out dogs,

and always, everywhere, an old
widow or widower trying to be dapper,
the woman with dust

on her nice little hat and too much
blush; the man in his brown shoes,
and gray pants an inch

too short: it gets me each
time, that whole inch missing. And oh,
what they carry:

his briefcase flat, flagrantly
useless, but something to hold on to—
her bag clasped around

her "just-in-cases" she never
leaves without: so much like what I
bring to this house—things, things

to hold on to in case night
freezes the shutters closed and only
my name remains on the mailbox.

The Off Season
Kathleen Graber

After Columbus Day, the shore towns close up so quickly
          no one bothers to pull in the signs. Postcards yellow
   all winter in windows beside a shell box, beside

t-shirts, plastic shovels, & pails. In my mother's house,
          I prepare to make things
                      disappear. I ask
   into the phone, *Who knew it would take so long*

to settle an estate? All around, the things she's saved have their say.
          But what do they say? Each day, they talk more & more
   only about themselves: red-lettered Chinese fortunes

in a drawer, as evocative as the dividend stubs around them.
          Fidelity Trust. An old dog will learn new tricks.
   My mother's x-rays. Months past their usefulness,

I still drive around with these images in my trunk:
          radiographs of the dead. *Memento mori*—
   who doesn't like the way it sounds? Or *uranium*?

Atomic number 92, that made these pictures possible,
                                all celluloid
          & *heft.* The off season: too early,
   too late, for anything you want to do. Afternoon's end,

that last curb before the street gives way to sand.
                            What can we say
          about our private sadness? The spine,
   its small white fists, three ribs around a fog of lung,

& her brain from every angle—although all the thoughts
          have gone. *You will visit a distant land.* Night:
   a rented film, or home movies on vacation

from the closet shelf in their little yellow Kodak cans. 1964.
              And my mother is *dressed,* as though life were
       an occasion, as though *fashion were the soul made visible*—

a claim that holds us because we want to prove all the ways
              it's flawed. I press rewind,
       & Annette Bening collapses again into hanger clatter—

not the last scene, but the almost over.
                             My niece
       safeguards my dead brother's ties in a plastic pouch
that travels with her. But when she opens it, is anything...

regained? The vanished other? The lost, un-see-able self? Alchemy,
              maybe, half memory, half
                                    silk.
       Marianne Moore's living room, her sofa, her phonograph,

the books on her shelf, in the order she put them,
              in their permanent place at the Rosenbach
       in Philadelphia. And there is a photograph there, too,

of the same room, before it was
                             moved. We have to keep
              checking ourselves. We're so tempted to play—
       the photo, the room, the photo... to keep on discovering

what's not there. My mother's heart was so strong I could see it
              beneath the blankets bang against the wall
       of her chest. I must have thought *a thing like that*

will just go on forever. Wind—the house rocks
              on its shallow footings—& home. What frightens me
       frightens me here
                      only a little less. The sky seems more.

The night-heron, duplicitous fisher, bends her long legs
              to the tide. The stars are brighter, but the dark fills up.
       The wise believe in magic. In a flicker, *poof,* my mother

pops up from below the water of a pool—& waves.
             We make the impossible possible; then
         it changes back. Somehow when we have to bury each other,

we do. She has become an Esther Williams bathing cap:
             wide white chin strap neatly snapped—
         around her head,
                     a rubbery halo of elaborate pink blooms.

Month Without a Moon
R. G. Evans

Any night I like, I can rise instead of the moon
that has forgotten us, not a thought of our sad lot,
and roam the darkened oblongs of the dunes.

Once you said the moon was some pale god
who turned away his face to cause the tides,
and once you said that, I of course believed

that you were mad. Now the ghost crab guides
me to the edge where land is not land, sea not sea,
and all the sky above is one dark dream.

This is the month with no full moon. You
were its prophet, and I am standing on the seam
between belief and what I know is true.

I gave you a diamond. It should have been a pearl.
It should have been a stone to hang above the world.

Why I Never Had a Baby
Barbara Daniels

I didn't have the right kind of quilt,
the one that's all illusion, as if
you could climb the steps of the pattern
to the stars. I had to string up

the flag each day, and that took
time, unfolding it in the required
way, then refolding it. Clouds
went by, and I had to watch them.

Have you seen the clouds puff up
like rising loaves of bread? I needed
time to collect the stamps
of Belgium, little earnest faces

tilting slightly, light dancing off
glasses, stamps with strange birds
that can't stop singing as if they're
crying, birds frozen in flight.

There's a Fire in the Distance
Emari DiGiorgio

Black smoke cloaks the sky. Even
in the desert we pray.

I'm used to eating with my hands now
and listen to the men I meet. I wish
I'd memorized one poem, having tired
of the same supplications.

They say there are a million ways
to kiss the earth; I don't think
this is one of them. We pull
our guns closer.

We wait for rain.

Hesitation Waltz
P. Ivan Young

I.

The gavotte is a 16th-century French dance,
the garotte a Spanish torture device.
The two terms are not unrelated. When the wire

tightens about the neck the crossing
of the feet imitates the folk tradition.
Country people gathered to dance the gavotte

just as they gathered to watch executions.
One woman of Dauphiné noted the swaying
of the corpse, the scissoring of the legs.

II.

The boy who hanged himself in gym class
seemed to dance the air as the coach struggled
to take him down. Dreadful pas de deux,

bearded face pressed to boy knees, toes flexing,
pointing. We had teased him for his softness,
his weight, the high-pitched voice. Later,

he recovered and hid the scar with a thick
gold chain. He walked the halls, shade of himself
like Beaumarchais in *The Ghosts of Versailles*.

III.

I straighten to the mirror, noose my tie in place
and think of you, danseur noble. The way two things
compress in a boy's body, love and death, the grace

with which you carried our words about your neck.
The way I danced an awkward farandole down
the galloping line, unsure of the beat, the teenage

bodies winding tight about me while my breath
dwindled, knowing you were watching us
from a door, almost afraid to lift my head.

Directions
Marcia LeBeau

Plant your feet on the ground. Put your hands on your knees. And whatever you do, don't try to explain this to anyone. (Not yet, at least.) When you are finished, open your eyes to an egg-white sky. You will have glistening skin and silk banners will line your mouth. Everyone will be talking too fast, making the banners bellow. You must take down the banners and fold them in quarters. Soon everyone's voice will return to normal. Except a young boy in Canton, Ohio who will ask you over and over why you're there. Either you'll answer him or pull the fire alarm. This will be the hardest decision you'll ever have to make.

When the Man You Love Is Blind
Ona Gritz

You can stop shaving your legs
when the temperature drops
and he'll say he likes a change
in texture with the seasons. You can
leave that bit of silver in your bangs.
Your fashion advice will be gospel.
When he tells you you're beautiful,
you'll know he's talking about
something in you that's timeless,
something about you that's true.
If, teasing, he says that smearing color
on your face is what a clown does,
explain how a touch of blush
can change the feel of entering a room
and he'll listen. He'll always listen
like the wide world is a raft with only
two people on it and he finds you
the more interesting of the two.
Imagine going with him to the Rockies.
He hears you sigh and asks
what the mountains look like. All you have
are words. *Awesome. Grandeur.*
But when you describe that feeling
of seeing your one life for the flicker it is,
he knows. *Oh,* he says. *Oh.*
It's like hearing music in a cathedral.

After Christmas, I Wreck My Knee
Again, Walking in Radburn Park
Svea Barrett

I was singing in the fresh air. It was strangely warm
for December. I was trying to sidestep the sadness
of the season. Holidays in our house have meant death—
my husband's mother, his brother, my son. I said no,
thanks, I'd go alone. It was just a puddle. I wore boots
and saw the sun ahead turning cedar hedges almost gold.

Who knew? Black ice beneath the water on the sidewalk
in this tame, New Jersey park—black ice like on the river
in those upstate New York winters back home in Beaver Falls,
the river we were warned against—how solid it appeared
and never was, how every winter someone looked across
and made a choice to ski, to snowmobile or step out on that
marbled, blackberry darkness with its creamy, dove-grey veins.

What did they see, the ones who did not listen,
as they danced almost across and disappeared?

Our Lady of the Highways
Pat Valdata

She stands in a field between monastery and interstate. At least
he thinks it's a monastery. Sometimes he thinks her eyes move,
following his progress north, like one of those paintings. Those eyes,

carved with such pity. Why should she pity? Why is she so damn sad?
Sons die. He knows. Get a life, lady. Shake off that mantle and hike up
your skirt. Jump off your pedestal. Feel the cold grass under the sole.

He wishes she would stretch her slim arms over her head, even if
she isn't really waving at him. One morning, a sleight of mist
made him see peripheral movement, but it was just a fox, trotting

across the field in front of her, something in its mouth—mouse,
vole. She looked down at it, arms spread, half question, half blessing.
Maybe she felt sorry for the vole. Or did she feel pity for the fox,

commuting to an empty den, needing to be a good provider, regardless.

Another Story
Dorianne Laux

Last night, watching another story of the murder of another woman,
a story we all know and can't seem to stop telling, the woman's daughter
was asked if she thought the murderer should receive the death penalty.

The daughter thought and thought and finally said she didn't know, couldn't
say. All she knew is that he should pay. When the cop showed her the ring,
charred black by the bleach, she held its gold zero up between her fingers.

The cop asked if she wanted to be hugged, and when she didn't answer said,
I have daughters. He'd worked on the case from the beginning, hadn't slept
for days, his eyes bagged, and I thought he might weep if she didn't let him

take her into his arms. *To be honest,* she said, tilting her face up to his,
I already knew. I could feel she was gone. The man who killed her mother
had made a *YouTube* video of a fly that landed on his finger. *Look,*

he'd whispered, *Look what we have here. What do you want little creature?*
His voice gentle, his face serene. *What have you come to tell me?*
She'd been dead for three days by then. *Who are we? Why are we here?*

Whose finger do we alight on to rest our tiny iridescent wings?
Whose job is it to speak to us with wonder, as if we were jeweled
creatures from another world: fragile, unlikely, alien beings?

Eyeing Male Pheasants in Alberta
Wanda S. Praisner

Clouds lift from snow-capped
Rundle Mountain.
Sun angles in through lace curtains
to a pair of stuffed pheasants.

I lop off the top of an egg
the way my father taught me,
spoon out the yolk,
scrape against shell
to remove the white...

Once they wanted to dilate, curette
my uterus to stop the bleedings,
but the hospital was full—
the child already two months inside me,
spared.

The owner pours coffee,
says the Gasthaus is patterned
after one in Bavaria. I tell him
my dad's from there, then quickly change
the tense for the first time—

like slipping down a gear on an icy turn,
he now at rest on a hillside
alongside the child who wasn't spared
a second time.

Outside, wind stirs the aspens.
I stare at the feathered breasts,
intricate overlappings—
glass eyes look straight out,
seeing as much as can be seen.

After You Left

Laura Anne Freedgood

Outside my window
the full moon of winter.

Trees lodge
in the hard earth.

A few brown leaves cling
like rusted ornaments.

The sun bows low
these days,

a fact, it seems,
impossible to change.

Pledge

Jan Goldman

Pledge me no more trivial conversation
No mix of this and that better left unsaid.

Pledge me the skeleton of things, the green heart
Show me the clean, clear center only in primary colors.

Pledge me a Japanese landscape
Everything simple to the point of abstraction or

Pledge me the sea, seen from the side of a sailboat
Corrugated surface of blue, its hidden depths
Flirting with sunlight.

Pledge me the outside of the outside
Let me find my own way in.

A Little Breast Music
Shirley J. Brewer

I was thirteen, flat-chested, and desperate,
until Rita Knipper's father, who knew
practically everything,
described television as the *boob tube.*

Armed with a tape measure and a *TV Guide,*
I commandeered the old red sofa
in front of the black-and-white screen,
where a miracle of invisible rays
would inflate my bust.

After endless episodes
of *Dragnet, Dr. Kildare,* and enough commercials
to boost me to a B-cup, and beyond,
nothing visible happened to my upper torso, yet
I did fall in love
with Liberace, his satin tuxedo
alive with a thousand points of glitter,
his music a wild jewel
pulsing in my chest.

Pump Your Own Gas

Laura McCullough

If Eddie Izzard and Tom Waits
fell in love, it would be in New Jersey,
home of the Boy Scouts and one of 36

states where sodomy is legal
except in Fort Dix and other military
bedrooms. Imagine the Luna Bell

Diner, Eddie in plaid—humor,
a dead giveaway—Tom fresh
from a fight with the Haitian

attendant on the Garden State
Parkway who wouldn't let him pump
his own gas. They'd agree on

Springsteen, order the Thomas Edison
Special—turkey with extra light
mayo and bright, pimento

filaments. About the future?
Eddie wants a flat in Ocean Grove,
Tom, a bungalow in Asbury Park,

a short walk to Fish Heads to sing
ballads for folks who still respect
The Blues. Ain't gonna happen. Izzy's

busy getting serious, and Tom, well,
New Jersey's just too small for a voice
that big. So it's up to us. Next time

you're in a diner along route 1 or 9,
Consider the resin chandelier, the quarter
jukebox. We've got all the music

and light this state can stand. Go ahead:
seduce someone with the one foreign
word you still know how to say.

Last Chance
David W. Worrell

Surprised, his shoulder receives
her shoulder's touch, the merest
brushing. They gaze at ocean's
glassy calm beyond the white-
bleached pilings, the seablasted pier.

Till now she'd known only faux
elegance, the Phoenix Marriott
where transported water, eerie blue,
filled the palm-lined, marble pool.

Her briny eyes caress the part
still left of him; he's a half-ruined
boat that she knows how to repair.

Unscrewing Eros
Lois Marie Harrod

after the photograph "Couple Entwined
on a Bed," by Henri Cartier-Bresson

Since she knows
a screw is just an inclined plane
wrapped in on itself,
she thinks unscrewing should be simple—
a matter of unwrapping the obvious,
her sex smoothed out like a sheet,
the spiral birthday ribbon pressed
to a fingernail, but then—his taut belly,
thigh tuned to the curve of her cheekbone,
the redolent helix of desire.
And then—his hair, so much of it,
unexpected and tangled in her own.

So she tries to remember the teacher who said
she wouldn't learn anything until she didn't
know what to do, until she couldn't fix the problem,
but what did fix mean? Stay or limit?

Maybe she should be grateful,
didn't the passion mags say hundreds
would like to be left where she is,
fast, held, the love goddess in a lover's arms,
netted fast by a gimpy nerd of a husband
who thinks he knows something
about the physics of love.

Yet something, she thinks, feels wrong:
she's no Aphrodite, he's no Ares,
there's no husband, not yet,
just this man, and sometimes she feels
as if she is merely stuck like that woman
who had her man on the high altar of God

and was stuck there a day and a night
and a day.

It's time to unwind,
but the screw is stronger than the nail.
This little twist may be holding the whole house together,
and weren't they both crazy over each other,
as two screwballs, lunatics, lovers
downing one madman after another?
And yet she was getting so tired,
stop, she wanted to say, just untwist our bodies,
let us come undone, let us lie
here, single and celibate,
all our organs fixed in canopic jars.

But then she was afraid that she
could undo everything, herself
the stone, the river, the sea,
that serpent, his pared apple,
untwist the spiral staircase to what? heaven?
yes, that could descend too
and leave her body a smooth plane
while whiffs of cirrus spun above.
Did she want that?

What You Learn to Say in French
Jin Ho Cordaro

You learn to link one small sound to another
after another, into a train gathering speed

You learn how to press the tip of your tongue against
the back of your teeth, and say
to your older brother, that you've watched him—
because speaking requires watching
You've heard his footsteps late at night,
and the front door close softly behind him.

You learn how to round your mouth, like blowing
a small ring of smoke, and say
to your mother that her love is like eating
one small potato all day.

Cherries

Michael Broek

That night you choked on the cherry
I thought about Chekhov, not right away
of course,   but later after
you had regained your breath, my skin
had stopped tingling, and you
had placed your eyes   back
into your head. Please, he has nothing
to do with this poem, just as he had
nothing to do with you in particular, but rather
I liked the sound of   *Chekhov's Cherry Orchard*
rolling around my mouth then forcing my tongue
towards a   certain   resolute   abstraction:
If you had died, I would have labored under
those trees—
a gardener, a magician of soil, a soothsayer—
reading futures in the forgotten spoils of fallen fruit.
        But you are fine, and I am still
slow to react, though full of verbosity,
planting trees where none need be,
harvesting cherries   two weeks late,
thinking pit trumps pith,
bones   over the flesh they endure,
how sweet your
throat
when it's full of longing.

In late summer the sea comes to the city
J. C. Todd

It isn't yourself you see at the end
Of August. You are a reflection in

A gutter's standing water, and the flat-you,
Swept up in traffic, an image, looking back.

The rush of drive time like the rush of surf
Just another noise fastened to the brain.

The faster the speed—ambulance, squad
Car—, the more headway into a boredom

Repetitious as sun that blunts and stuns
Until all seagulls look the same. Generics.

The oddness of it, being hollowed by
Not being able to notice detail.

Imagine—what is it like to be left
With a solitary thought, uprooted,

Embodiment unmoored, pulled out from
Beneath you by unfathomed undertow?

Every last cell lost. In this way
You learn distance from your memory.

The Crowd at the Gates
Stephen Dunn

The crowd had gathered by the gates.
Like most crowds, it was more shifty
than intelligent, on the verge
of dangerous. At times it undulated
like gelatin, at others its movements
were barely perceptible, as if it were
waiting for some kind of permission.
A crowd, the gates knew, was a tsunami
in the making. Which is why the gates
were needed—big, stolid, iron gates
clear about their mission. The crowd
had gathered by them, and the gates
feared someone would make a speech.
The gates always feared the articulate
appeal to a collective deprivation.
The gates had experience. They knew
that after such speeches, crowds lack
a sense of humor, which can diffuse
misery, literally make a crowd break up.
Behind the gates was the stronghold,
in which the deciders made their decisions.
The gates would try to protect them,
regardless. The crowd was getting larger,
swaying now. Someone began to speak,
and for a moment the gates wondered:
If it were possible for us to be moved,
might we, also, be outraged, want to open
ourselves wide, and say, *Take them?*

Love Songs
Douglas Goetsch

At 12 Richard Perry came from California
to throw a football way farther than anyone
on the block. If that's the kind of thing
you admire—and we did—you could also
admire other things about him, even his stutter,
which manifested in the huddle when he drew
plays on his man-sized palms, his intelligent eyes
signaling some clever maneuver moments
before the words for it emerged, creating
a kind of charmed suspense while the defense
waited hands on hips. I was his favorite receiver,
always going long, all through the fall, winter,
into spring, where one day, after several blinks,
Richard stated the following: "Love songs
are the best songs there are." Four 12 year olds
looked at each other, then back at Richard,
who broke the huddle without a play.
Later we would find out he had a girl—
Regina Meiselbach, from the other side
of the highway—and though his assertion
about love songs seemed way out of line,
isn't it always the case with that kind of feeling,
that you have to tell everyone? Personally
I found love songs boring and stupid, like
watching my parents play bridge, but that
was also his point: to tell us something
we couldn't know. And I wish now I could
have surrendered to something the way
Richard Perry gave it up completely,
something I didn't do at age 12 or 20
or even 40. I've never shocked anyone
with a confession that strange and tender,
stuttered without embarrassment because
he had love, he had Regina and a song

in his head that he knew was worth more
than his rocket arm which could launch
footballs into the sky. And in case you
haven't figured it out this is all about you.
You, my love, spiraling into my arms
like a pass that's been traveling 30 years,
like a song I can finally hear.

TV Comes to Logan, West Virginia
Kathleen Corcoran

The freight elevator clanks and clatters
and my father tells me we'll ascend
on through the warehouse roof
and into sky then sail across the hills.
But we stop instead at 5th-floor furniture
with modern dinettes for fifties families,
rows of plastic-covered chairs,
and the first shipment of Motorola TV sets.

When he'd come home from selling furniture
to coal company stores up Buffalo Creek,
he'd produce Tootsie Rolls from air
and pull them from behind my ears,
chanting "Holla Molla Hot Die, Spinna Majig."

Now my magician turns a knob creating
voices, laughter from a wooden box,
a black-and-white confetti of swirling dots.
And there's the shadow of a face.

In a warehouse he conjures a new world,
our own Show of Shows that plunges
from sky and zooms across mountains—
a flash descending, lighting our dark hollow.

Seneca on Friendship

Benjamin Paloff

No pressure, Lucilius, but I hang around this life
to see how you'll fare against the monstrous appetite
of the hippocampus and the flimsy outboard called "Rescue."
By the time you learn that ideology is a question
of how you deal with unauthorized personnel, it's too late.
I cannot help being larger than your life. As the path
from the sea carries you through the low mountains
and another pre-electrified night, it's all I can do to hold back
the need to take you down. I'm watching you now,
upright and small, never to lose your way.

Cape May, January
Mary Olmsted Greene

The earth will shrug us off—
but first, split the oak, tend the fire.

The earth will shrug us off—
but first, get your paints, render the sky.

Green surface of the earth
tugged down by the weight of monastery walls,

Green surface of the earth
obliterated by the white worms of blizzards.

The earth will crack at its polar edges
and we'll be as shells, smashed

to bits, hardening to glass. But first—
the fog is lifting. Waves break, shapely and silver.

A young girl holds a white cup.
She is about to begin.

Falling in Love with Fire
Donna Vorreyer

First, the stove—"Don't touch—hot"
the admonition, followed by a slap
on the hand, a healthy brand of fear.
But the lights went out so often in
that old house on Pierce that I was
taught to strike the match, its pungent
sulfur sucked like a drug into my nostrils.

Then the bonfires at Folger Park, a band
of gangly boys and girls feeding flames
built by the river. We'd sit so near that
our flesh would smell of smoked meat,
sparks sputtering on our swimsuits. When
the heat got too intense, the rubber soles
of our shoes gooey, we'd kick them off,
wade into the water where we stoked

a different kind of blaze, each hand
and tongue singeing its signature on
my skin, my mother's voice billowing
in my brain, reiterating the danger of
proximity. But this new warmth bloomed
in my bones, and despite the warnings,
I danced my flame from wick to wick,
ignited an inferno impossible to dismiss.

Later I learned the shock of backdrafts,
but even this knowledge could not halt
the seeking of the slow boil, the frantic
flush, could not stifle the belief that one
can get this close and escape unscathed,
that burning does not always lead to ash,
as I imagine even an ant must enjoy the
first, focused rays of the magnifying glass.

Home Remedy 1968
Shawn Regina Jones

Debris had fallen months
before my unwanted arrival
when Grandmother gave
her unwed daughter
tar black pills to swallow
behind Tanqueray Gin,
mixed turpentine and hot water
in a pea green bucket,
held mom's flannel gown
around her stretched waist,

and told her to crouch down
as close as she could get.

the unruly and the dead
Cindy Savett

                               we
the unruly and the dead
gather sticks
form acres of swaying hills

steal hinges off iron
doors   whisper
into the morning cup of silence

        I fling my hands from the rail

and the hot boil
of air
hums incessantly in my ears

                you have mold on your aging eyes

                      empty pots
                      fill your balcony

Breathing Under Water
Catherine Doty

Florida's just a thumb on a jigsaw puzzle,
but under water the Weeki Watchee Mermaids
pour their tea, cook, exercise, iron clothes, guzzle
with muscular skill their Grapette soda,
with only occasional surreptitious sucks
on an air hose hidden in shell-studded scenery.
They grin, open eyes afloat in their blue-lit skulls.
Holding my breath was a skill I practiced, too,
like when I was ten years old and woke to a body
lowering onto my body, and a breath that put me in mind
of a rotten leg, a thing I'd seen in a book once
and which scared me, but not as much as this body
on top of my body, these jabbing fingers. I was wildly aware
that the room I was in was a pigsty, and I was a pig to be sleeping
in my clothes, and I wanted to blame it on someone, which
would have meant speaking, which I could not do—
it would have been too real—and I was too old to blame anyone
anyway. I closed my eyes to make the black world
blacker. The lamp was within my reach, and a railroad spike
I could easily have lifted, and also a bowling ball I'd found
on the tracks, but all I could think of was being ashamed
and dirty, and grateful the whole thing was happening
in black and white, like those mermaids on TV, their lips
and nails a black I knew was red, their long white legs
safely fused in their glistening tails.

Sermon
Karen Zaborowski Duffy

That's what my father sounded like he was giving
on Sunday when he preached the difference
between horseshit and bullshit.

Horseshit is what all ministers are full of,
but bullshit is what they're praying for.
Most people are stuck with dogshit and pigshit

doesn't count *which you'd already know*
if you'd been paying attention.
This was what my father was pacing over

when I got home from Sunday School
where I was sent to be less like him.
This was Sunday in my house, Dad simmering

along with Mom's pot roast, the smell of onion
soup mix hanging in the air on all split levels.
Nobody called it depression back then.

At the table he'd ask for collard greens and turkey
necks, not that he was from the South, because
Texas is not the South, it's the West, like I said before.

And sometimes he'd tell boyhood stories of
outhouse-tipping and watermelon-stealing
on his way to school with his colored friend,

Punk White, who was not really his friend, because
Jesus Christ, he was just the colored boy up the road.
But I said in 1930 it was against the law in Texas

for whites and coloreds to go to school together.
But that was the best example of bullshit he ever heard.
Nobody needs a goddamn law to tell you no self-respecting

colored boy would go to school with us. They didn't want to.
He told me this. He told himself this.
I walked to school. Punk walked to school.

We both walked to school together
at the same time. His school was next to ours,
right next to ours, well, not right next to ours,

close. But not too close. They got the same books,
the same exact books. They got our books
when we were done with them.

That was the punchline. That was him saying
this story ends with a punchline.
When I consider my father, I wonder how

long a person can tell a story
that's supposed to be funny after he knows
it isn't. He told what he could stand to hear

himself telling, which worked until
he boiled over with the bulk of the century
and Punk's loss. His loss.

Years of being friends and not
being friends, of making excuses to go
to Punk's on Sunday. Corn pudding

for Miss Ida, or Miss Ida's calico beans for him.
Years of being separated by a fence
made from planks of wood and

nailed together, maybe set on fire.

[Perhaps by comet.]
Paul-Victor Winters

Perhaps by comet.
Perhaps a gnashing of subterranean teeth.
And then, perhaps, The Virgin of Guadalupe, unabashedly
          fitful, heralding the world's collapse.

Perhaps implosion.
Or the brimming sea, imposing itself upon a newly-hewn shoreline.
Or all the ancient prophecies come to be at once.

And all our luck run out, simply.
Or something like that: all four horsemen, seven bowls
          and seven seals, eruption of lava and ash.

Perhaps we'll fall to plague or chemical evil.
The center, then, will fail to hold.
And then the denouement.
The end.
And then, the then.

Shore Town, Winter
James Richardson

Now that it's January
in Victorian New Jersey,
the aqua and magenta
gingerbread of triple-deckers
is past incongruous, way past forlorn,
and all the way to the Grand Canyon's
weird silence,

the loud absence
of the forces of improbable scale and precision
that must have made this
(and what a job to paint it!)
for their very own,
then flip-flopped down the boardwalk
and out of the galaxy,

leaving the sea,
pretty calm this evening,
the tide trending in,
the moon and sun, this winter twilight,
just about equally dim.

When Matthew Arnold settled one elegiac hand
on a pale shoulder, gesturing out
over the Channel, he saw France
quietly letting go its light.
This is America, we see nothing
but size, sky and ocean
working on gray-green
not much of anything,

though in this later century
we, also, hear the *grating roar,*
mixed maybe with a syringe or two

and indestructible packing, but never mind,
the hiss and click
of calciferous debris that Arnold heard
Sophocles hear as human misery.

Waves in themselves, turning to her,
he whispered (and I whisper)
are huge but powerless.
Their megatons
collapsing on a single shell
leave it unfazed,
but hardness of touch, quickness of suspicion,
the quickening step
past pain:
shells break, we break, each other.
Ah love, etcetera.

Weary of detail,
Arnold's particular deity
has chilled out to think about the Big Picture,
and on his darkling plain
they've closed the stores,
as if in a day or two
his sun will go red giant
and scrape the planet down to the stone.

But the Sea of Faiths
in the broadest sense is doing
just fine, thank you. Endlessly it reproduces
Taco Bells and Jiffy Lubes
along our hardening arterials.
Not a day goes by
without the world recording
zillions of world records,
no day that our collective résumés
fail to add a zillion lines,
and those who declare
for Higher Things enrich
in desert compounds the uranium
of Zeal's white glare.

Over and over,
just when it seems we're blessedly
running out of gas,
idiot saints
figure out how to make money
from going on just as before.

Ah love, the news is old
that the wind slides through carless lots
and slaps flat on chainlink:
more than a century,
now, it's been the end of the world,
and this long, long twilight,
this last *Alas,* has lost its power
either to frighten or console.

On a similar shore
You and I are old, Ulysses crooned
but then again
'Tis not too late to seek a newer world.
We call it a day,
heading for Parkway North,
not too downcast to be lifted
by a car absurdly loud with teens
and a music that drowns ours
as they pass us, entering

this paused flick
of dark hotels and meters on Expired
hoping for solace and a Sign! a Sign!
and sure, if anything is sure, to find
both less and more than we have found
on a winter Sunday
in the flickering neon
of this new old new old world
that says *No Vacancy* and means
We are empty, and we plan to stay that way.

APPENDIX A

For even more supplemental material, go to murphywriting.com/anthology.

Fortunes

No need to worry! You will always have everything that you need.
Delay is the antidote for anger.
A romantic evening awaits you tonight.
You will make a sudden rise in life.
Be discreet. It will pay off.
Appreciate those you admire, but forge your own path.
You eyes will be opened to a world full of beauty, charm and adventure.
What you left behind is more mellow than wine.
A thrilling time is in your immediate future.
You have an active mind and a keen imagination.
Over self-confidence is equal to being blind.
You are capable of dispelling others' doubts.
Your love of gardening will take on new meaning in your life.
You radiate goodness.
A modest man never talks of himself.

Random Quotations

"Glory is fleeting, but obscurity is forever."
– *Napoleon Bonaparte*

"Victory goes to the player who makes the next-to-last mistake."
– *Chessmaster Savielly Grigorievitch Tartakower*

"Don't be so humble—you are not that great."
– *Golda Meir, to a visiting diplomat*

"People demand freedom of speech to make up for the freedom of thought
which they avoid."
– *Søren Aabye Kierkegaard*

"Grant me chastity and continence, but not yet."
– *Saint Augustine*

"Only two things are infinite, the universe and human stupidity, and I'm not
sure about the former."
– *Albert Einstein*

"I find that the harder I work, the more luck I seem to have."
– *Thomas Jefferson*

APPENDIX B

New Jersey Facts and Trivia
from a 2003 prompt, adapted from www.50states.com/facts

– New Jersey is the state with the highest population density in the U. S.: An average 1,030 people per square mile, which is thirteen times the national average.

– In November 1914, the New York Tribune, cooperating with Bertram Chapman Mayo, founder of Beachwood, New Jersey, issued an "Extra" announcing: "Subscribe to the New York Tribune and secure a lot at Beautiful Beachwood. Act at once, secure your lot in this Summer Paradise now!"

– New Jersey is the only state where all its counties are classified as metropolitan areas.

– North Jersey is the car theft capital of the world, with more cars stolen in Newark than in any other city.

– In order to meet the increasing demand for his wire rope, John A. Roebling opened a factory in Trenton, New Jersey in 1848. John and his sons built a suspension bridge across the gorge of the Niagara River, the Brooklyn Bridge and many other suspension bridges in the U.S.

– John P. Holland designed, built, and tested the first submarine in the Passaic River in New Jersey.

– Jack Nicholson, Bruce Springsteen, Bon Jovi, Redman, Paul Robeson, Naughty by Nature, Sugar Hill Gang, Jason Alexander, Queen Latifah, Judy Blume, Susan Sarandon, Aaron Burr, Alexander Hamilton, Whitney Houston, Eddie Money, Frank Sinatra, Grover Cleveland, Woodrow Wilson, Walt Whitman, Bruce Willis, William Carlos Williams, Allen Ginsberg, and Meryl Streep are all New Jersey natives.

Truth, Lies and Honesty

"Oh what a tangled web we weave, / When first we practise to deceive!"
   – Sir Walter Scott

"A lie gets halfway around the world before the truth has a chance to get its pants on."
   – Sir Winston Churchill

"Truly, to tell lies is not honorable;
  but when the truth entails tremendous ruin,
  To speak dishonorably is pardonable."
  – *Sophocles*

"Truth is generally the best vindication against slander."
  – *Abraham Lincoln*

"There are few nudities so objectionable as the naked truth."
  – *Agnes Repplier*

"Believe those who are seeking the truth. Doubt those who find it."
  – *André Gide*

"All truth passes through three stages. First, it is ridiculed. Second, it is violently opposed. Third, it is accepted as being self-evident."
  – *Arthur Schopenhauer*

Time

"Tempus fugit (time flies)."
  – *Ovid*

"It was the best of times, it was the worst of times...."
  – *Charles Dickens*

"We must use time as a tool, not as a crutch."
  – *John F. Kennedy*

"Time is a fixed income and, as with any income, the real problem facing most of us is how to live successfully within our daily allotment."
  – *Margaret B. Johnstone*

"There is time for everything."
  – *Thomas Edison*

"I wasted time, and now doth time waste me."
  – *William Shakespeare*

"Time heals all wounds, unless you pick at them."
  – *Shaun Alexander*

"Time may be a great healer, but it's a lousy beautician."
  – *Unknown*

Einstein Says...

"The secret to creativity is knowing how to hide your sources."

"The release of atom power has changed everything except our way of thinking... the solution to this problem lies in the heart of mankind. If only I had known, I should have become a watchmaker."

"The intuitive mind is a sacred gift and the rational mind is a faithful servant. We have created a society that honors the servant and has forgotten the gift."

"The monotony and solitude of a quiet life stimulates the creative mind."

"It has become appallingly obvious that our technology has exceeded our humanity."

"Everything that is really great and inspiring is created by the individual who can labor in freedom."

"You teach me baseball and I'll teach you relativity.... No, we must not. You will learn about relativity faster than I learn baseball."

"Life is like riding a bicycle. To keep your balance you must keep moving."

"So long as there are men there will be wars."

"Nationalism is an infantile disease, the measles of mankind."

"I believe in standardizing automobiles, not human beings."

"I love to travel, but I hate to arrive."

"Politics is more difficult than physics."

"Lasting harmony with a woman (was) an undertaking in which I twice failed rather disgracefully."

"I don't believe in mathematics."

"We have to do the best we can. This is our sacred human responsibility."

"I have no special talents. I am only passionately curious."

APPENDIX D

Money

"A billion here, a billion there, pretty soon it adds up to real money."
– *Senator Everett Dirksen*

"A bank is a place that will lend you money if you can prove that you don't need it."
– *Bob Hope*

"If all the rich people in the world divided up their money among themselves there wouldn't be enough to go around."
– *Christina Stead*

"A successful man is one who makes more money than his wife can spend. A successful woman is one who can find such a man."
– *Lana Turner*

"Advertising may be described as the science of arresting the human intelligence long enough to get money from it."
– *Stephen Leacock*

"Everybody likes a kidder, but nobody lends him money."
– *Arthur Miller*

Television

"Television is a new medium. It's called a medium because nothing is well-done."
– *Fred Allen*

"Television is now so desperately hungry for material that they're scraping the top of the barrel."
– *Gore Vidal*

"Television is more interesting than people. If it were not, we would have people standing in the corners of our rooms."
– *Alan Coren*

"Seeing a murder on television... can help work off one's antagonisms. And if you haven't any antagonisms, the commercials will give you some."
– *Alfred Hitchcock*

"Television has done much for psychiatry by spreading information about it, as well as contributing to the need for it."
– *Alfred Hitchcock*

APPENDIX E

The Odyssey

"Travel reminds us we are always traveling."
  – *James Richardson*

"As you journey through life, take a minute every now and then to give a thought for the other fellow. He could be plotting something."
  – *Hagar the Horrible*

"A tourist is a fellow who travels thousands of miles so he can be photographed in front of his car."
  – *Émile Genest*

"A journey of a thousand miles begins with a single step."
  – *Lao Tzu*

"Anything you fully do is an alone journey."
  – *Natalie Goldberg*

"The longest journey is the journey inward."
  – *Dag Hammarskjöld*

"There are only two emotions in a plane: boredom and terror."
  – *Orson Welles*

"Nothing is so awesomely unfamiliar as the familiar that discloses itself at the end of a journey."
  – *Cynthia Ozick*

"Every path may lead you to God, even the weird ones."
  – *Real Live Preacher*

"The journey is the reward."
  – *Chinese proverb*

"On life's journey faith is nourishment, virtuous deeds are a shelter, wisdom is the light by day and right mindfulness is the protection by night. If a man lives a pure life, nothing can destroy him."
  – *Buddha*

"Every woman is like a time-zone. She is a nocturnal fragment of your journey. She brings you unflaggingly closer to the next night."
  – *Jean Baudrillard*

Moon lines from **A Moon for the Misbegotten,** *by Eugene O'Neill*

"If you got him alone tonight—there'll be a beautiful moon to fill him with poetry and loneliness...."

"And you, Josie, please remember when I keep that moonlight date tonight I expect you to be very sweet to me."

"...I'd give a keen of sorrow or howl at the moon like an old mangy hound in his sadness if I knew how, but I don't...."

"...A drink or two will make me better company, and help me enjoy the moon and the night with you...."

"Let's sit down where the moon will be in our eyes and we'll see romance."

"Everything is far away and doesn't matter—except the moon and its dreams...."

"...Sure, even the moon is laughing at us."

"...I don't like your damned moon, Josie. It's an ad for the past."

"...You were mostly quiet and sad—in a kind of daze, as if the moon was in your wits as well as whiskey."

"Are you going to moon at the sunrise forever, and me with the sides of my stomach knocking together?"

Moon Myths

– February 1865 is the only month in recorded history not to have a full moon.

– The moon is actually moving away from the earth at a rate of 1.5 inches per year.

– Only about fifty-nine percent of the moon's surface is visible to us here on earth.

– The moon is not round, but egg shaped with the large end pointed towards earth.

– The earth rotates at about 1,000 mph. By comparison, the moon rotates at about 10 mph.

– Moonrise takes place about fifty minutes later each day than the day before.

– The new moon can't be seen because the illuminated side faces away from the earth. This occurs when the moon lines up between the earth and the sun.

Moon Facts

– Some people act crazy due to the pull of the full moon.
– The moon disappears during certain days of the month.
– The moon is a living creature or a god.
– The moon is made of green cheese.
– The moon and the sun chase each other across the sky.
– There are men or other creatures living on the moon.
– The moon is pulled across the sky by a person, animal, or force.
– There is a man in the moon.
– During a full moon, some people turn into werewolves. Ha Ha!

Moon Words and Phrases

"To the moon, Alice!"	Moon pie
Casting beyond the moon	Moon blindness
Crying for the moon	Moonbeam
Honeymoon	Mooncalf
It's all moonshine	Moonglade
Loony	Mooning
Lunacy	Moonlighting
Lunatic	Moonrakers
Mock moon	Moonrat
Moon about	Moonshine

My Bad

"America is a mistake, a giant mistake."
　– *Sigmund Freud*

"A life spent making mistakes is not only more honorable, but more useful than a life spent doing nothing."
　– *George Bernard Shaw*

"If I had to live my life again, I'd make the same mistakes, only sooner."
　– *Tallulah Bankhead*

"In a few minutes a computer can make a mistake so great that it would have taken many men many months to equal it."
　– *Unknown*

"A good many young writers make the mistake of enclosing a stamped, self-addressed envelope, big enough for the manuscript to come back in. This is too much of a temptation to the editor."
　– *Ring Lardner*

"The real hero is always a hero by mistake; he dreams of being an honest coward like everybody else."
　– *Umberto Eco*

"She had an unequalled gift... of squeezing big mistakes into small opportunities."
　– *Henry James*

Success/Failure

"I don't know the key to success, but the key to failure is trying to please everybody."
　– *Bill Cosby*

"If at first you don't succeed, failure may be your style."
　– *Quentin Crisp*

"Failure is not the only punishment for laziness; there is also the success of others."
　– *Jules Renard*

"A thinker sees his own actions as experiments and questions—as attempts to

find out something. Success and failure are for him answers above all."
  – *Friedrich Nietzsche*

"You always pass failure on the way to success."
  – *Mickey Rooney*

"Many of life's failures are people who did not realize how close they were to success when they gave up."
  – *Thomas Edison*

"Success is the ability to go from one failure to another with no loss of enthusiasm."
  – *Sir Winston Churchill*

"We have forty million reasons for failure, but not a single excuse."
  – *Rudyard Kipling*

"All you need in this life is ignorance and confidence; then success is sure."
  – *Mark Twain*

"The secret of success is sincerity. Once you can fake that, you've got it made."
  – *Jean Giraudoux*

"Why be a man when you can be a success?"
  – *Bertolt Brecht*

"Nothing fails like success."
  – *Gerald Nachman*

"Nothing succeeds like the appearance of success."
  – *Christopher Lasch*

"We must believe in luck. For how else can we explain the success of those we don't like?"
  – *Jean Cocteau*

"Sometimes I worry about being a success in a mediocre world."
  – *Lily Tomlin*

"The penalty for success is to be bored by the people who used to snub you."
  – *Nancy Astor*

Random Dance Terms

Adagio – Any dance to slow music; also, part of the classical *pas de deux* in ballet.

Alegrías – A form of flamenco dance. It suggests the movements of the bullfight. It originated in Cádiz, Spain and literally means "joys."

Allegro – A dance with a fast or moderate tempo. The part of a ballet class comprised of fast turning or jumping that usually follows the adagio.

Arrastre – To drag.

Assemble – A jump from one to both feet.

Bunny Hop – A "party dance" that is a variation of the conga line.

Cocktail Samba – A combination of Ballroom Samba and Brazilian Samba.

Étoile – French for "star." Also, the highest rank a dancer may hold in the Paris Opera Ballet.

Fandango – A lively Spanish dance traditionally accompanied by castanets or clapping. The dance usually begins slowly and increases greatly in tempo.

Line – The length and stretch of the body from head to toe.

Line of Dance – The counterclockwise course followed by dancers progressing around a room.

Milonga – A Spanish dance that originated in Andalucía before traveling to other regions. In Buenos Aires, the Gauchos danced it in a closed position in the lower class cafés. Their interpretation of the dance emerged into what today is our Tango.

Par Terre – Refers to steps performed on the floor, as opposed to *en l'air*.

Paradas – Stops.

Port de Bras – Literally "carriage of the arms." A movement or series of movements of passing the arm or arms from one position to another. Also used to denote exercise designed to develop the upper part of the body.

Suzy Q – A dance step in the Lindy Hop, Big Apple, Salsa Shines, and other dances. It is also known as the Grind Walk.

Tack Annie – A step used in the Shim Sham Shimmy.

APPENDIX I

Clown Wisdom

Charlie Chaplin

"I remain just one thing, and one thing only, and that is a clown. It places me on a far higher plane than any politician."

"All I need to make a comedy is a park, a policeman and a pretty girl."

"In the end, everything is a gag."

Rodney Dangerfield

"I told my psychiatrist that everyone hates me. He said I was being ridiculous—everyone hasn't met me yet."

"When I was a kid my parents moved a lot, but I always found them."

"I haven't spoken to my wife in years. I didn't want to interrupt her."

"My wife is always trying to get rid of me. The other day she told me to put the garbage out. I said to her I already did. She told me to go and keep an eye on it."

Groucho Marx

"A clown is like aspirin, only he works twice as fast."

"Outside of a dog, a book is man's best friend. Inside of a dog it's too dark to read."

"I've had a perfectly wonderful evening. But this wasn't it."

"No one is completely unhappy at the failure of his best friend."

W. C. Fields

"Last week, I went to Philadelphia, but it was closed."

"'Twas a woman who drove me to drink, and I never had the courtesy to thank her for it."

"Once, during Prohibition, I was forced to live for days on nothing but food and water."

"Horse sense is the thing a horse has which keeps it from betting on people."

Insect Common Names

alderflies
ambrosia beetle
antlions
ants
Asian tiger mosquito
asparagus fly
bed bug
boll weevil
bugs
butterflies
cabbage bug
caterpillar
centipede
chalcids
cicadas
grasshoppers
greedy scale
house fly
ichneumons
Japanese rice leaf miner
June bug
juniper webworm
katydids

lacewings
larch sapwood beetle
leafhoppers
leek moth
lone star tick
mangrove scarab beetle
pharaoh ant
plant hoppers
potato bug
praying mantis
red bollworm
red imported fire ant
sawflies
scale insects
scorpion flies
stink bug
strawberry tortrix
turnip moth
wasps
western flower thrip
wheat stink bug
whiteflies
winter moth

APPENDIX K

Furniture

Types

armoire	dresser	settee
bean bag	escritoire	side chair
bench	fauteuil	sideboard
bookcase	folding table	sofa bed
buffet	footstool	sofa table
cabinet	four poster bed	stool
camelback sofa	gateleg table	table
canopy bed	grand piano	tuffet
chaise lounge	headboard	tuxedo style chair
chest	highboy	upright piano
coffee table	hutch	vanity set
credenza	kneehole desk	wardrobe
curio	love seat	watchman's chair
drawing board	secretary	wing chair

Styles

Jacobean (1600 – 1690)
Early American (1640 – 1700)
William and Mary (1690 – 1725)
Queen Anne (1700 – 1755)
Colonial (1700 – 1780)
Georgian (1714 – 1760)
Pennsylvania Dutch (1720 – 1830)
Chippendale (1750 – 1790)
Robert Adam (1760 – 1795)
Hepplewhite (1765 – 1800)
Federal (1780 – 1820)
Sheraton (1780 – 1820)

Acknowledgments

Grateful acknowledgment is made for permission to reprint the following works:

"After Christmas, I Wreck My Knee Again, Walking in Radburn Park," from *I Tell Random People About You,* by Svea Barrett. Copyright © 2011 by Svea Barrett. Used by permission of the author and Spire Press, Inc.

Laure-Anne Bosselaar, "Follen Street," from *Small Gods of Grief.* Copyright © 2001 by Laure-Anne Bosselaar. Reprinted with the permission of the author and The Permissions Company, Inc. on behalf of BOA Editions Ltd., www.boaeditions.org.

"A Little Breast Music," from *A Little Breast Music,* by Shirley J. Brewer. Copyright © 2008 by Shirley J. Brewer. Used by permission of the author and Passager Books.

"Cherries," by Michael Broek. First published in *The American Poetry Review,* Vol. 40, No. 4, July/August 2011. Copyright © 2011 by Michael Broek. Used by permission of the author.

"TV Comes to Logan, West Virginia," by Kathleen Corcoran. First published in *Loch Raven Review,* No. 4, 2008. Copyright © 2008 by Kathleen Corcoran. Used by permission of the author.

"What You Learn to Say in French," by Jin Ho Cordaro. First published in *Flywheel Magazine,* No. 1, 2011. Copyright © 2011 by Jin Ho Cordaro. Used by permission of the author.

"Why I Never Had a Baby," by Barbara Daniels. First published in *The Dos Passos Review,* Vol. 6, No. 1, Spring 2009. Copyright © 2009 by Barbara Daniels. Used by permission of the author.

"There's a Fire in the Distance," by Emari DiGiorgio. First published as "Letter" in *U.S. 1 Worksheets,* Vol. 55, 2010. Copyright © 2010 by Emari DiGiorgio. Used by permission of the author.

"Breathing Under Water," by Catherine Doty. First published in *TLR: The Literary Review,* Vol. 53, No. 1, Fall 2009. Copyright © 2009 by Catherine Doty. Used by permission of the author.

"The Crowd at the Gates," from *Here and Now: Poems,* by Stephen Dunn. Copyright © 2011 by Stephen Dunn. Used by permission of W. W. Norton & Company, Inc.

"After You Left," from *Slant of the Heart,* by Laura Anne Freedgood. Copyright © 2010 by Laura Anne Freedgood. Used by permission of the author and Pudding House Publications.